EXPLORING BOSTON HARBOR

EXPLORING BOSTON HARBOR

With Photographs and Text

By

ALAN MIKAL

THE CHRISTOPHER PUBLISHING HOUSE
NORTH QUINCY, MASSACHUSETTS 02171

PRINTED IN

THE UNITED STATES OF AMERICA

*To my
Mother and Father*

PREFACE

At first I began exploring the islands of Boston Harbor out of curiosity, hoping to find buried treasure or to discover ancient, unrecovered relics. Then, I found myself returning to them again and again, fascinated perhaps, but mostly to enjoy the quiet serenity of their location. It seems as if each individual island created its own unique and mystical atmosphere through both history and natural beauty. My impressions of each island were so marked and varied that I felt they should be recorded in figurative language and with picturesque photography. Historically, Boston Harbor deserves as much recognition as any landmark in Massachusetts. From a naturalist's point of view, the islands represent the true heart and soul of New England itself. Their wild vegetation and abrupt rock formations characterize the landscape of the Northeast Coast and are unparalleled anywhere in this vicinity.

There have been many varied proposals for the future development of these islands. Presently, they lie dormant, awaiting their reawakening to usefulness. Therefore, this book is an attempt to familiarize the people with their history, and make them aware of the wild, untamed beauty of the islands, so close by, in Boston Harbor. It should be stressed here, however, that regardless of progress and future development, it is of prime importance to convince the public that all historic landmarks should be conserved for posterity, and that the natural beauty of some of the islands be retained, unchanged and unmolested by civilization.

At this point, I would like to express my deep appreciation to Mr. Edward Rowe Snow, Boston's famed Marine

Historian. Through thorough research and notable writing, he is responsible for bringing the islands of Boston Harbor to the attention of the general public. I am particularly grateful to him for this, because his many books and articles helped formulate my interest in the Harbor. They not only stimulated my interest, but also brought out the adventuresome spirit in my heart, a spirit which each of us possesses to some degree. No sooner had I read his volumes, than I found myself exploring every nook and cranny of the individual islands. I consider Mr. Snow the modern day "founder" of Boston's historic harbor, and I feel that his lifelong interest should be brought to further attention and carried on in the future.

Alan Mikal

CONTENTS

ILLUSTRATIONS

BOSTON HARBOR

Geologists believe that originally Boston Harbor did not have any islands. They conjecture that the islands were underwater cliffs and shoals that emerged after the glaciers of the Ice Age melted and receded. At that time, the islands were much larger than they are today and the harbor was relatively smaller. Eventually, the forces of the ocean and the wind eroded the mainland, hollowed out the harbor, reduced the size of the islands and carried the sand and the silt southward to form a large arm of land known today as Cape Cod.

The first discoverer of Boston Harbor is unknown. It can only be assumed that the explorers who founded the continent of North America may have seen this bay. The Norsemen and Vikings, who traveled south from Greenland, are alleged to have been the first to visit this continent. Leif Ericson, the son of the Viking chieftain Eric the Red, is credited with an unrecorded discovery of North America, while his brother Thorwald, is said to have anchored his ship in Boston Harbor.

Although Columbus, an Italian, is recognized as the discoverer of America, he never traveled farther north than Puerto Rico and Cuba. Actually, the main part of North America was explored by the English. In 1497, while seeking a route to the Indies, the Englishman John Cabot landed at Cape Breton, Nova Scotia. A year later, he navigated the east coast of North America. His discovery formed the basis for England's eventual claim on this land. Another explorer who came to the new continent was Bartholomew Gosnold, an Englishman. In 1602, he investigated the areas between Nar-

ragansett Bay and Cape Elizabeth, Maine. He is also credited
with having named Cape Cod because of its abundant cod-
fish. In 1605, Samuel de Champlain, a Frenchman, landed in
Canada, founding the Province of Quebec. He, too, explored
the region between Nova Scotia and Cape Cod and drew the
first detailed chart of the New England Coast. These explorations eventually led to the permanent settlement of the land.

The east coast of America was divided into two sections.
The area of New England was known as "Northern Vir-
ginia" and everything south of that was called "Southern
Virginia" or simply "Virginia." In 1607 Captain John Smith
established the first permanent settlement in America at
Jamestown, Virginia. Later that same year, Sir Ferdinando
Gorges, a British soldier, and Sir John Popham, the Lord
Chief Justice of England, organized the settlement of "North-
ern Virginia." The attempt at colonization by Popham's
brother, at the mouth of the Kennebec River in Maine, failed.
Smith, however, continued his explorations of the east coast
and, in 1614, named the region of "Northern Virginia," "New
England" because of its similarity to his motherland. The
first permanent settlement of "New England" occurred in 1620
when the Pilgrims established the Plimoth Bay Colony in
Plymouth, Massachusetts.

In 1621, Captain Miles Standish and a group of Puritans
explored Boston Harbor. Accompanying Standish were an
Indian guide named Squanto (Tisquantum), for whom the
Town of Squantum was named, William Brewster, a preacher
at the church of the colony, for whom the Brewster Islands
were named, and Isaac Allerton, the Deputy Governor of
Plimoth, after whom Point Allerton in Hull was named. In
addition, the group included William Trevour, who claimed
Thompson's Island for David Thompson.

The early colonists came to Boston Harbor frequently in
the ensuing years to trade with the Indians and, eventually,
they settled the land. In 1622, Thomas Weston attempted a

Seagulls on Mussel Bed—Thompson's Island

settlement at Wessagussett, now Weymouth, Massachusetts. However, he abandoned it a short time later. Also in 1622, Sir Ferdinando Gorges and his partner, Captain John Mason, received a grant, by royal charter, to the region of New England situated between the Merrimack and Kennebec Rivers. In 1629, they divided the area between themselves. Gorges acquired the Province of Maine and in 1639 became its first governor, while Mason obtained New Hampshire. Both of these colonies were under the rule of Massachusetts until New Hampshire became a separate royal province in 1679 and Maine became the twenty-third state in 1820. However, in 1623, following the original acquisition by Gorges and Mason, another settlement was established in New Hampshire. David Thompson, who was employed by the "Council for New England," settled at "Little Harbor," New Hampshire, at the mouth of the Piscataqua River. This settlement was located near the present day city of Rye, New Hampshire. Thompson had also been granted an island in Boston Harbor that is today known as Thompson's Island, to which he later moved. In the same year, 1623, Robert Gorges, the son of Sir Ferdinando Gorges, unsuccessfully tried another settlement at Wessagussett.

Reverend William Blaxton (Blackstone), who had accompanied Robert Gorges to Wessagussett, remained behind after Gorges' departure and established the first permanent settlement on the peninsula of Boston in 1625. This area was known as "Shawmut," an Indian phrase for "living waters," because of the abundant freshwater springs located there. It was also referred to as "Tramount" or "Trimountain" due to the presence of three consecutive hills called Pemberton, Beacon and Mt. Vernon. Today, only Beacon Hill remains; the others were leveled for building and filling purposes. Blaxton's house was located on Beacon Hill near the present intersection of Beacon and Charles Streets. Also in the year 1625, Samuel Maverick built the first house in Chelsea, Massachusetts, known then as "Winnisimmet," at the approximate location of the Chelsea Naval Hospital. In addition, Captain Wollaston and Thomas Morton landed in Quincy, Massachusetts, and called their settlement "Mount Wollaston" which was later changed to "Merie-Mounte." These various men formed the first permanent settlement of Boston and its environs.

After David Thompson left his colony at the Piscataqua River in 1626, he settled on what is now known as "Thompson's Island" in Boston Harbor. When William Trevour claimed the island for Thompson in 1621, he called it "Island of Trevour." However, Thompson named it after himself when he moved there. His trading post, erected to barter with the Indians, was the first permanent establishment in Boston Harbor. In 1630, the Massachusetts Bay Company, led by Governor John Winthrop, colonized "Shawmut." They landed first at Charlestown but, due to the lack of fresh water there, they soon moved to "Shawmut." Shortly thereafter, they renamed the area "Boston." By 1635, the General Court of Boston had granted the islands in Boston Harbor to various towns and persons. In the ensuing years, the islands changed hands many times among individuals, towns, cities and the Federal Government.

Topographically, much of the inner harbor has been filled in since the arrival of the first settlers. The City of Boston, located in the Charles River Basin, was originally a peninsula barely larger than the present community of Squantum, Massachusetts. East Boston and Logan Airport span what was once four islands, "Noddle's," "Governors," "Bird" and "Apple" Islands. The area known as Orient Heights, between Chelsea and Winthrop, was originally Hog Island (sometimes referred to as Breed's Island). Deer Island became part of Winthrop, Massachusetts. Present-day South Boston was located in the area once known as "Dorchester Neck." On the mud flats to the northeast of this neck, called "Dorchester

Flats," wharves and piers have been erected that jut out into the "Main Ship Channel."

Boston's waterways have undergone considerable change over the years, making them more suitable for maritime purposes as well as for providing additional land for the area's growing population. I imagine that the early explorers and settlers would not recognize Boston Harbor if they were to visit it today. There is, in fact, nothing so constant in life as change.

Seagull's Nest—Outer Brewster Island

THE BREWSTER ISLANDS

Millions of years ago, the four Brewster Islands are believed to have been a single huge land mass. Evidence of this stems from the fact that in low tide, three of the islands in the Brewster chain are joined together by shallow sandbars. It is thought, that over the ages, the ocean has eaten away at the land, dismembering it and eventually forming four separate domains.

This group of islands was named in 1621, after Elder William Brewster, a preacher at the church of the Plimoth Bay Colony. He had come to Boston Harbor on an excursion with Captain Myles Standish, Isaac Allerton, a crew of ten, and Squanto, their Indian guide. During this exploration, Point Allerton in Hull was named after Isaac Allerton, the Brewster Islands were named for William Brewster, and the island of Squantum was named for Squanto. After Brewster's death in 1641, the Town of Hull acquired title to the Brewster Islands. Later, in 1686, John Loring, a resident of Hull, purchased them and was the last to hold claim to all four islands simultaneously. After his passing, each island was sold separately and developed its own history.

The Brewsters are located in Suffolk County, and are the easternmost islands in the harbor. They are windblown, surf-beaten, hard-core islands, consisting of crude land that provides little shelter for their inhabitants. It is difficult to conceive of men and their families trying to civilize and cultivate this land. But men, like the birds, want to be free and were bold and determined enough to test their endurance on such harsh terrain. At present, these islands are all uninhabited, used only by hordes of seagulls as a natural refuge.

Middle and Outer Brewster as seen from Great Brewster Island

GREAT BREWSTER ISLAND

Great Brewster Island is composed of two hills, one large and the other small, connected by a shallow valley of marsh land. The northeastern bluff rises to 104 feet in height, catching the force of easterly gales that eat away at its side, causing minor landslides of pebbly sand to fall into the pounding surf below. The etches of erosion are clearly visible on its slopes. This northern bluff gently dips into a tidal gulley called Greater Brewster Plain and continues upward into another, much smaller hill, the southwestern bluff. Overall, the land of Great Brewster covers twenty-three acres.

Prior to the construction of Boston Light on Little Brewster Island, the Town of Hull erected a small range-light on Great Brewster's northern bluff in 1681. After Boston Light was put into service, the range-light was no longer used and subsequently was demolished. However, its approximate location can be determined by a water well that was dug near the range-light by Boston Light's second keeper, Captain John Hayes, in 1726.

The island has been owned privately as well as by both the City of Boston and the United States Government. In 1774, John Jenkins owned Great Brewster and gave it to the Second Baptist Church. The church leased the island to several tenants, one of which was James Brackett of Quincy, who moved there in 1817. The City of Boston purchased the land in 1848 and the United States Government constructed a seawall on its northeastern shores, to prevent erosion by the sea. Later, in 1875, the city leased the island to Benjamin Dean, who moved his house there from Long Island. However, by 1900, there were no inhabitants on the island. Dur-

21

ing World Wars I and II, the United States Government took possession of the island, and erected fortifications on Great Brewster to protect the entrance to Boston Harbor. Remnants of these forts are still visible.

Oddly enough, this island has had only one shipwreck to scar its shores; that of the Clara Jane in 1898, in which no lives were lost. Presently, an abandoned barge sits marooned at the base of the great northern bluff. Great Brewster Island, at this writing, is privately owned and, being the largest in the Brewster chain, it takes on a "big brother" image, looking over the lesser members of this Boston Harbor Island family.

Great Brewster Island

Erosion on Northeast Bluff—Great Brewster Island

Great Brewster Plain

Wild Dandelion—Great Brewster Island

MIDDLE BREWSTER ISLAND

Of all the harbor islands, Middle Brewster is the least accessible. Nary a cove, a narrow stretch of beach, or even a minute inlet can be found to gain access to its twelve acres of land. Approaching its rocky shores, surrounded by jutting underwater cliffs and sharp abutments, one can't help but recall Ulysses' ancient sirens standing on the shore, luring unaware sailors to a watery death with their sweet songs. Steep slopes of weathered sand, fastened to the base rock by crude beachgrass, like spikes hammered halfway into the soil, add to the insurmountability of the island. Evil-looking, vulturous birds with long, gray-brown necks and sharp, black beaks, which appear to be a breed of the Cormorant, stalk the island's viny wooded area. Once on Middle Brewster, the explorer cannot help but feel a vague uneasiness with each movement heard in the underbrush.

Originally, in 1719, Middle Brewster was called "Bridges Island" by its first private owner, Mr. Loring of Hull, because it spanned the water between Greater and Outer Brewster Islands, somewhat like a bridge. In 1759, it was named "Gould's Island" after its owner, John Gould. Finally, it became known as "Middle Brewster Island," simply because of its location directly between Greater and Outer Brewster Islands. During the mid-1800's, fishermen's huts dotted its slopes and abundant fish and lobsters were trapped and caught among the craggy rocks just off the shore. Between Middle and Outer Brewster Islands lies a channel bearing the name "Flying Place." It is said to resemble a boiling cauldron during northeast gales because of the whitewash created by the waves pounding against the rocks and boulders. These treacherous rocks pierce the surface of the water in low tide, but are dangerously submerged in high water. They are strewn across the entire width of the channel, making it virtually impassable. In 1828, a ship named the "Fachin" was wrecked when it tried to scurry through the passage during a storm. It was trapped between the underwater cliffs, which acted like the pincers of a lobster squeezing the life out of its helpless prey, and it sank to the bottom almost immediately.

Augustus Russ, founder of the Boston Yacht Club, settled here in 1871 and erected a small villa on the southwestern cliff. The crumbled foundation is still there, its bricks lying helter-skelter among the weeds. A solid stone arch stands intact near the foundation. It looms as the symbolic door to defeat at the hands of the elements, which most islanders inevitably encountered.

Melvin Adams purchased the island around 1892 and allegedly inscribed a tablet in memory of both Russ and his crude dwelling. Subsequently, Mr. Whitney bought Middle Brewster from Adams and lived on the western shore. A flagpole is said to have been found near his house bearing the words "Erected by Richard S. Whitney in 1902." [1] Edward Rowe Snow claims to have found an old book in the cellar of Whitney's house containing clues to a buried treasure located on Chatham Beach, Cape Cod.

Nearly impregnable, the island joins the ranks of all the Brewster Islands as being lonely, yet savagely beautiful. Although still privately owned, it has no tenants except for the wind, the gulls and a pervading desolation.

---

[1] Snow, Edward Rowe, *Romance of Boston Bay* (Boston: Yankee Publishing Co., 1944), p. 222.

Stone Arch—Middle Brewster Island

Old Foundations—Middle Brewster Island

Outer Brewster Ledges

OUTER BREWSTER ISLAND

This island, located the farthest out to sea in Boston Harbor, is also part of the Brewster chain. It has a rugged terrain and presents a most challenging and carefree character. Because of its isolation and natural formations, it is, perhaps, the most beautiful of all the harbor islands. Beyond its eastern shore lie the unknown perils of the vast Atlantic. Its seventeen acres present the first barrier in the harbor encountered by the powerful partnership of wind and sea, converting their brute gales into a pulpy spray. Even on the most serene days, one can hear the harsh noise of the waves lapping against its shores, tossing fragments of driftwood upon the beach and polishing its mighty cliffs. Seagulls of the most courageous character inhabit this island, piercing the windy sky with their shrill cries. Their sounds are very different from those gulls which follow fishing boats into port, begging for their catch. These are shrieks of warning to trespassers from an entirely different breed of gulls, which are wild and free. They are gentle unto themselves but are savagely cruel to predators, unafraid to protect what is naturally theirs.

Although this land has been called "Outward Island," it is more commonly known as "Outer Brewster Island." A seawall was never built around Outer Brewster, as on most of the other islands, simply because it has been preserved by its own sheer cliffs. These abutments have been magnificently shaped and molded by the roaring surf and are said to surpass, in beauty and grandeur, even the renowned cliffs of Nahant, Massachusetts.[1] It is a bleak, bare island without a

---

[1] Shurtleff, Nathaniel B., *Topographical and Historical Description of Boston* (Boston: Rockwell and Churchill, 1891), p. 575.

single tree rooted in its soil. In 1776, however, one small tree was perched on the eastern tip and was appropriately named "The Eastern Most Tree in the Harbor!"

Nathaniel Austin owned Outer Brewster in 1817 and, later, his brother Arthur acquired rights to the island. Both men, during their lifetimes on this barren outpost, quarried its granite rock which they sold as building material in Boston. Granite from Outer Brewster Island was used in the construction of a building still standing in Charlestown Square,[2] and also in the paving of Eliot Street in Boston.[3] Beautiful geometric contours are visible on the cliffs and ledges from where the granite was taken by these men. Also, Arthur Austin created one of Outer Brewster's two distinguishing landmarks. He attempted to cut a narrow channel directly across the island, so that boats could pass through, or weather storms in the sheltered cove at the channel's entrance. Although he never completed his endeavor, his extensive work is readily identifiable. The other landmark is "Pulpit Rock," located on the northwestern side of the island. This rock is so named because when the sharp winds of northeast gales sweep over its flat top, they are said to "deliver a powerful sermon" of loud, mournful moans.[4] Actually, when viewed from the summit of the island's eastern slope, its shape resembles a minister's pulpit. Also, on the southern side of the eastern slope, there are rock formations that look much like the pipes of a giant church organ.

An unfortunate incident occurred on this island when one of its later owners, Mr. Jeffers, drowned during a storm while fishing in his dory just off of its shore. In 1871, Benjamin Dean had possession of the island and he, in turn, sold it to Freeman Degaust in 1909. The United States Government

---

[2] Sweetser, Moses Foster, *King's Handbook of Boston Harbor* (Cambridge, Mass.: Moses King Corp., 1882), p. 249.

[3] Snow, Edward Rowe, *Romance of Boston Bay* (Boston: Yankee Publishing Co., 1944), p. 225.

[4] Sweetser, *op. cit.*, p. 249.

Austin's Channel—Outer Brewster Island

Rock Formation—Outer Brewster Island

purchased the island in 1913 and erected fortifications to defend Boston Harbor during the First World War. Years later, in 1941, Battery Jewel was built and still stands as a proud monument representing Outer Brewster's services during World War II.

At present, Outer Brewster Island is privately owned. However, the Metropolitan District Commission hopes someday to convert it into a public recreation area. People with a hearty spirit of adventure will enjoy exploring the scenic wonders of this isolated paradise.

Pulpit Rock—Outer Brewster Island

CALF ISLAND—LITTLE CALF ISLAND

Directly to the north of Great Brewster Island is a small, seventeen-acre outpost known as Calf Island. It has a relatively flat surface of crude granite rock covered with weeds and high grasses. Several small beaches nestle between ominous ledges and are accessible by boat. Snugly situated in the middle of this island is a shallow, fresh-water pond that is entirely encompassed by tidal marshlands. During the hot summer days, a thick mist rises above the pond's calm surface creating ghostly images as it swirls in the gentle breezes. Just off the northern shore of the island lies another rocky piece of land, barely one acre in area. It appears to have been joined at one time to its larger neighbor and, therefore, is called Little Calf Island. It stands futile and forgotten, providing only a safe and untouched refuge for hordes of seagulls. It has never served any purpose for man throughout its history and has never been settled.

Calf Island was once known as "Apthorp's Island," although the origin of this name is uncertain. Allegedly, it received its present title from Robert Calef, who was a merchant in Boston. He is best remembered for his book, *More Wonders of the Invisible World*, which helped to calm the hysteria of witchcraft that had gripped New England in the latter 1600's. The first recorded owner of Calf Island was Lieutenant Gould, whose son later acquired rights to Middle Brewster Island. In 1845, Calf Island was owned by a man named "King" Turner, who eventually became the keeper of Bug Light at the western end of Brewster Spit. He was reputed to have been a very tall, burly well-built man, with a long shaggy beard that covered most of his face. His awesome physical appearance earned him the appellation of "The King of Calf Island." [1]

In the years that followed the Civil War, lobster fishermen came to this island to carry on their trade. The small, wooden shelters which they built on the shores, however, have long since fallen and washed out to sea. In 1891, Benjamin Cheney and his wife, Julia Arthur, who was an actress, moved to Calf Island from their previous home on nearby Middle Brewster. Later in 1902, Cheney purchased Calf Island and built a large house on the abrupt southwestern cliffs facing Great Brewster. Today, only the foundation and two brick chimneys remain intact, silhouetted against the sky. The initials "B.P.", probably for Benjamin P. Cheney, are found inscribed over the hearth of one of the chimneys. The United States Government acquired the rights to the island during World War I. Many years later, prior to the outbreak of World War II, Charles Quigg proposed that a huge, recreational area be built on Calf Island. His plans included a marina, swimming pool, golf course, tennis courts and a hotel. The United States Government, however, retained the rights to the land until the end of the Second World War, and Quigg was never able to fulfill his dream.

Sometime during the island's early history, a passenger ship washed up on its shore. Neither the name of the vessel, nor the date of the wreck is known. It is believed that the drowned crew members were buried by fishermen on the island in unmarked graves. Thus, Calf Island has sometimes been referred to as "The Home of the Lonely Grave." [2]

---

[1] Rideing, William H., "The Gateway of Boston," *Harper's Magazine* (August, 1884), p. 360.

[2] Snow, Edward Rowe, *Romance of Boston Bay* (Boston: Yankee Publishing Co., 1944), p. 224.

Calf Island

Foundation of Julia Arthur's Home—Calf Island

At present, both Calf and Little Calf Islands lie within the boundaries of Suffolk County and are privately owned. The texture of their landscapes seems less rugged than the terrain found on the Brewster Islands. Only the remains of Cheney's villa suggest any historical past on Calf Island, while the legend of the "Lonely Grave" lends to it a mysterious atmosphere.

Skeletal Remains of Trees—Calf Island

GREEN ISLAND

Green Island lies just to the north of Little Calf Island. Barely two acres in area, its terrain is bleak. It is strewn with rocks and dotted with dwarfed vegetation that consists of scrubby bushes and weeds. There are no trees because the soil is sparse, shallow and not fertile enough to nourish any deep roots. It is a relatively inaccessible island, lacking beaches and safe landing sites.

Originally, Green Island was part of the Brewster chain and was known as "North Brewster Island." It is named after Joseph Greene, a merchant in these waters during the mid-1700's, who frequently visited its shores. Aside from the few rickety fishing shanties that have roosted briefly on its banks over the years, only one courageous soul ever dared to make Green Island his permanent home. That individual was Samuel Choate, a hermit, who moved here in 1845. He built a crude hut out of driftwood and lived in it for many years, thriving on the island's loneliness. In 1851, Choate was evacuated to the mainland when a treacherous storm hit Boston Harbor; he returned, however, and stayed until his death in 1865.

Now, and probably forever, Green Island will remain a refuge for seagulls. Its only faithful visitors are the whistling wind, the birds that soar above it and the sea that washes its shores. There are no traces to be found either of Choate's home or of the fishermen's huts. Presently, Green Island is privately owned, but remains a barren and isolated outpost in Boston Harbor.

Rangelight Ruins—Lovell's Island

LOVELL'S ISLAND

Lovell's Island, situated directly to the northeast of George's Island, is the flattest island in Boston Harbor, spanning an area of approximately sixty-two acres. It is distinguishable by two long, sandy beaches running almost parallel to each other, located on opposite sides of the island. The water on the western shore is deep, and on a calm day, crystal clear. When Henry David Thoreau visited this bay on his journey to Cape Cod, he described the water as being extremely cold and pure. It could easily be mistaken for fresh, country, spring water. This beach is easily accessible to most craft in either high or low tide, because, located just beyond its shore, is the "Narrows Channel" that passes between Gallop's and Lovell's Islands. Protruding from this beach toward this channel is a relatively new pier, whose sturdy appearance is a welcome sight for sea-weary boatsmen.

The eastern beach is not as easily accessible. Only at high tide can a boat reach its shores, for it is barricaded by the "Ram's Head Flats," a vast stretch of rocky mussel beds which extend for several hundred yards out into the bay in low tide. Exposed to the harsh east winds, its shores readily accumulate whatever debris or treasures the sea may choose to wash in. Both the eastern and western shores are striking in their natural beauty and comparable to any of those on sandy Cape Cod.

This island was named around 1630, after Captain William Lovell, a resident at that time of the Town of Dorchester and a merchant in Boston. The City of Charlestown acquired the rights to Lovell's Island in 1648, but transferred them to the Town of Hull in 1654. After Hull relinquished its possession, Elisha Leavitt and his grandson, Caleb Rice, of Hingham, each owned the island successively. In 1825, the United States Government purchased the island from Rice.

Two tragic shipwrecks have occurred off the treacherous shores of Lovell's Island. In 1782 the "Magnifique," a French man-of-war, under the command of Admiral Vaubaird, struck a protrusion of the "Ram's Head Flats" on the northeast shore, now called the "Man of War Bar." The shoal pierced the woody flesh of the vessel, causing it to sink almost immediately, carrying with it a cargo of gold and silver which has never been recovered. Over the years, the endless process of erosion caused by the waves washing incessantly over the sand, has covered the wreck completely, so that today it lies in a grave, buried deep under the island itself, some fifty feet inland. Only timber from its hull has been retrieved while its treasure remains lost, perhaps forever. Just four years later, in 1786, during a severe winter storm, a passenger ship was hurled upon these same treacherous flats. The passengers, forced to seek shelter from the cold winds, fled to the summit of the island's only hill where they hid behind a huge boulder. The next morning all were found, dead from exposure, still huddled behind the rock. A young man and his bride were found locked in each other's arms, frozen to death in the icy grips of the storm. Since then, this boulder has been appropriately named "Lover's Rock." Although presently overgrown with weeds, the rock still bears witness to the prevailing comfort of love in the face of death. It is discernible for some distance offshore, and is a prominent island landmark on the western point.

When the Government purchased Lovell's Island in 1825, a seawall and breakwater were constructed on the northeastern rim to protect it from erosion. Later, in 1900, a fortification, called Fort Standish, was built by the United States War Department. In 1902, two small lighthouses were erected on the northern side of the island. Remains of the fort and of one range-light can still be found. Legend has it that the light-

Lover's Rock—Lovell's Island

Fort Standish—Lovell's Island

house-keeper and an associate found buried treasure in the ground adjacent to the light, perhaps that of the "Magnifique." A hole several feet deep was dug by them in search of this treasure. Curiously enough, even today, there is a large excavation near this site that may well have been their "treasure hole." One point of interest regarding Lovell's Island made by the historical novelist Edward Rowe Snow alleges that a tunnel runs underwater from Lovell's to George's Island.[1]

At present, the island is under the jurisdiction of Suffolk County and is owned by the Metropolitan District Commission for the promotion of recreation and conservation. Its beaches provide a perfect location for family outings as well as for endless exploration.

Lovell's Island

---

[1] Snow, Edward Rowe, *Romance of Boston Bay* (Boston: Yankee Publishing Co., 1944), p. 217.

GEORGE'S ISLAND

George's is the most easily identifiable island in Boston Harbor because of its massive, concrete fortress. Its land mass comprises twenty-eight acres and it is one of the most historic sites in the City of Boston.

Originally, in 1628, it was called "Pemberton Island" after its first rightful owner, James Pemberton of Hull. Later, around 1710, the island acquired its present title from Captain John George, a prominent Boston merchant. Elisha Leavitt and his grandson, Caleb Rice, both of Hingham, each owned the island until Rice finally sold it to the United States Government in 1825.

Crude defenses were constructed on the island in 1778, to protect the French fleet of Count D'Estaing, anchored off of Peddock's Island from the British warships prowling the outer harbor. The French were enemies of the British, because they had backed the Colonists during the Revolution. Also, the two empires were constantly battling over territorial acquisitions elsewhere. The French dismantled the cannon from their ships and placed them on the northeastern side of George's Island. These cannon, mounted on dirt piles, appeared so ominous and forbidding that the surprised British soon fled to safer waters and the French, as well as the City of Boston, were saved from attack.

The United States Government purchased the island in 1825 and shortly thereafter, in 1833, began construction of Fort Warren. This fort was named for Major-General Joseph Warren, a physician as well as President of the Provincial Congress, who was killed in the Battle of Bunker Hill in Charlestown. The walls of this fort were constructed of granite,

quarried from Quincy and Cape Ann and are approximately
sixty-nine feet high and eight feet thick, enclosing an area
of about twelve acres. It has a pentagonal shape similar to
that of Fort Independence on Castle Island, and originally
held three hundred guns. The fort is surrounded by a dry
moat fifty feet wide, and is spanned by a drawbridge at the
main entrance. It took seventeen years to complete this bas-
tion. Fort Independence and Fort Warren were designed and
built simultaneously by General Sylvanus Thayer of Braintree, Massachusetts. Thayer served a long term as superintendent of the United States Military Academy at West
Point, and although he was not its first superintendent, he
is called the "Father of West Point." Also, Thayer Academy,
a private school in Braintree, is named in his honor.

During the Civil War, Fort Warren was under the command of Colonel Dimmick. A trooper stationed there at this
time, composed the renowned song "John Brown's Body,"
more commonly known as "The Battle Hymn of the Re-
public," which was later sung by the Second Infantry or Tiger
Battalion. Murals commemorating this song are painted on
the walls of the island chapel. Many confederate prisoners
were brought to Fort Warren and confined within its dark
"Corridor of Dungeons" or in other parts of the fort. Among
the more prominent prisoners were James M. Mason and
John Slidell, both of whom were commissioners, representing the confederacy abroad. They were captured at sea while
en route to London, England. Alexander Hamilton Stephens,
the vice-president of the Confederate States, was also imprisoned here. Each of these important figures occupied
rooms just to the right of the fort's main entrance. Fort Warren was known as the "Yankee Bastille" [1] for it was comparable to the "French Bastille" in Paris, France, because
both of these fortress prisons became infamous during politi-
cal upheavals in their respective countries.

---

[1] Sweetser, Moses Foster, *King's Handbook of Boston Harbor* (Cambridge,
Mass.: Moses King Corp., 1882), p. 235.

George's Island

Entrance to Fort Warren—George's Island

A popular tale lends a mysterious atmosphere to Fort Warren. It is known as the legend of "The Lady in Black." As the story goes, a southern lieutenant was imprisoned at the fort during the Civil War. His wife came to George's Island and attempted to free him; however, during the escape, she was caught and subsequently hung. It is alleged that her last request was to die in woman's clothing since she had come disguised as a man. Accordingly, she dressed in a long, black cloak for the execution. It has long been rumored that she still inhabits the "Corridor of Dungeons," haunting the place where her husband was held captive; many people even claim to have seen her spirit prowling the island on several occasions. Some of the dungeons are open to the public and a plaque and stairway at their entrance mark the ghost's hideaway. Her legendary presence makes exploring the confines of this fort both eerie and exciting.

Fort Warren was active in the Spanish-American War, as well as in both World Wars. The fort's glory lies entirely in its historic past. M. F. Sweetser, in his book, *King's Handbook of Boston Harbor*, commemorated this island fortress as "a garrison that is concentrated United States—an island of pure nationalism." In days gone by, Fort Warren of George's Island and Fort Independence of Castle Island created a pair of "stony knuckles" [2] in Boston Harbor, through which an approaching vessel had to pass before reaching the well-protected port of Boston. Presently, the island is located in Suffolk County and it is owned and operated by the Metropolitan District Commission primarily for recreational purposes. Recently, on May 31, 1972, a plaque was erected on George's Island designating it as a National historic site. Earlier, in 1970, the fort was recognized as a National historic landmark by the United States Department of the Interior.

---

[2] *Ibid.*, p. 239. (quote by Thoreau)

Gun Emplacement and Parade Ground–Fort Warren

Gulls on Sunken Barge—Gallop's Island

GALLOP'S ISLAND

Almost every island in the harbor has been named for some figure prominent in the history of Boston or its environs. However, new names could easily be adopted for each of these islands, describing their present appearances. Gallop's Island was named after John Gallop, a well-known sea captain in these waters around 1650. He was also a famous "Indian Fighter" and the captain of Boston's first pilot boat. Nonetheless, a more appropriate title for the island would be "The Isle of Many Buildings," in honor of the many structures which once graced its horizons, but are now levelled to their very foundations. Strewn about the underbrush are concrete blocks, bricks and cement patios battling the weeds for a place on the island. Those foundations that were too solidly constructed to be overrun by the grasses, lie exposed, providing a resting place for the island's seagulls. To be sure, the bleakness of these decayed edifices creates an eerie atmosphere on Gallop's Island; after all, they were once active dwellings, inhabited for a time, and then for a variety of reasons were gradually abandoned and left to decay into a ghost-town of a by-gone era.

The name of this island has been frequently misspelled in government documents, written as Gallup's Island; the true spelling, however, is Gallop. The island is shaped like a "leg of mutton" [1] and covers an area of sixteen acres. A narrow range of land emerges from the southeast side of the island, forming the paw of the leg. At its tip, called "Peggy's Point," [2]

---

[1] Shurtleff, Nathaniel B., *Topographical and Historical Description of Boston* (Boston: Rockwell and Churchill, 1891), p. 545.

[2] Snow, Edward Rowe, *The Islands of Boston Harbor 1630–1971* (New York: Dodd, Mead and Co., 1971), p. 158.

stands a beacon that warns ships passing through the "Narrows Channel," of shallow water thereabouts. The main part of the island constitutes the haunch of the leg, upon which are located numerous stark foundations scattered throughout clusters of stunted trees.

From the early 1600's through the latter 1800's, this land was used primarily for farming because of its rich soil. Vegetables and dairy products produced here were transported across the bay to the mainland to be marketed in nearby cities. Various individuals owned this farmland until 1860, at which time the City of Boston purchased it from a Mr. Charles Newcomb. During the Civil War, fortifications were erected on the island by the United States Government and up to 3,000 men were quartered in its barracks.

After the Quarantine Hospitals on Rainsford and Deer Islands ceased to function, a new quarantine station was constructed in 1866, on Gallop's Island. Gallop possesses the largest cemetery of all the islands because its Quarantine Hospital remained in continuous use longer than any other, until 1937. Its burial ground contains approximately two hundred and forty-eight graves, mostly those of fever victims. At the present time, these graves are barely visible beneath the heavy undergrowth of bushes and weeds. In 1868, a seawall of granite was built by the United States Government on the northeastern bank to prevent erosion.

Following the closing of the Quarantine Hospital on Gallop's Island in 1937, the buildings were used as a training center for sea-rescue units, as well as a radio school run by the United States Maritime Service. The sea-rescue center closed shortly thereafter; the radio school, however, remained in operation until the end of the Second World War. Only in recent years have the buildings on the island been neglected and allowed to fall into decay.

Gallop's Island is located in Suffolk County and is privately owned. It seems to lie dormant awaiting its reawakening to a more useful function once again.

Gallop's Island

Old Pier at Gallop's Island

Breakwater in Fog—Gallop's Island

NIX'S MATE

Located just to the north of Gallop's Island is a huge black and white cement pyramid perched on a square, granite base. This unusual looking structure was built in 1805 and marks the place where an island known as Nix's Mate was once located. Its major land mass was washed away by the eroding forces of the wind and the sea, leaving behind a rocky sandbar visible only in low tide.

In 1636, John Gallop, for whom Gallop's Island is named, was granted the rights to Nix's Mate Island and used its twelve acres as a pasture for his sheep. Both his ownership and the existence of the island are verified in an excerpt from a legal document:

> "There is 12 acres of land granted to John Gallop, upon Nixes Island, to enjoy, to him and his heirs forever, if the island bee so much." [1]

During the seventeenth century, several pirates who were convicted and executed in Boston for their crimes, were transported to Nix's Mate for burial. Two pirates, Samuel Cole and Henry Greenvill, were buried on Nix's Mate; a third, William Fly, was hung there in chains and left to rot, serving as a warning to other pirates. An excerpt from a 1726 Boston "Newsletter" describes the incident.

"On Tuesday the 12th Instant, about 3 p.m. were executed here for Piracy, Murder + c. Three of the Condemned Persons mentioned in our last, viz. William Fly, Captain, Samuel Cole, Quartermaster, and Henry Greenvill, the other viz. George Condick, was Repriev'd at the Place of Execu-

---

[1] Snow, Edward Rowe, *The Islands of Boston Harbor 1630–1971* (New York: Dodd, Mead and Co., 1971), p. 92.

tion . . . Fly behaved himself very unbecomingly even to the last; however advised Masters of Vessels not to be severe and barbarous to their Men, which might be a reason why so many turned Pirates. . . . Their bodies were carried in a Boat to a Small Island called Nick's Mate, about 2 Leagues from the Town, where the abovesaid Fly was hung up in Irons, as a Spectacle for the warning of others, especially Seafaring Men; the other two were buried there." [2]

Nix's Mate acquired its name from one of two sources. An old legendary tale states that a Captain Nyx was killed by his first mate while sailing into Boston Harbor. The first mate was hung on this island for the crime, but before his execution he allegedly shouted, "I shall prove to you all that I did not kill the Captain, for this island shall wash away to show my innocence." [3] Another probable origin of its title came from a Dutch phrase "Nixie Shmalt" which translates, "The Wail of the Water Spirits." It describes the sound of the waves breaking on the island shore as heard by a Dutch crew that sailed into the harbor in the early 1700's. The phrase was pronounced as "Nix-iesh-malt" and was finally translated as "Nix-his-mate." [4]

The pyramidal structure that marks Nix's Mate Island was erected by the Boston Marine Society and stands approximately twenty feet high, atop the twelve foot granite base. It has been determined that the disappearance of the island was due not only to erosion but also to the removal of slate, used as building material in the City of Boston. Another island, called Bird Island was also used as a burial place for pirates, and was likewise washed away from its original location in Boston's East End. It presently constitutes a portion of Logan Airport.

---

[2] Campbell, J., *Boston Newsletter* (July 14, 1726), p. 1172.

[3] Sweetser, Moses Foster, *King's Handbook of Boston Harbor* (Cambridge, Mass.: Moses King Corp., 1882), p. 197.

[4] Sweetser, *op. cit.*, p. 198.

Nix's Mate

Rainsford Island

RAINSFORD ISLAND

Of all the islands in the harbor, Rainsford Island's eleven acres have the most gentle topographical contours. Essentially, it is comprised of two small plots of fertile soil, connected by a low-level, rocky isthmus. The eastern bluff of this island gradually ascends from a broad meadow, located at its base, to a plateau from which most of the harbor is visible. The meadow is partially shaded by a small grove of trees that continue a short distance up the side of the slope. The western head, on the other hand, is relatively flat except for a very slight incline. Just off the western bank lie four consecutive sets of craggy rocks called the "Quarantine Rocks," so named for the two quarantine fever hospitals that were formerly located on Rainsford Island. Three of the groups of rocks are submerged in high tide, presenting a hidden hazard in the path of unaware yachtsmen. However, they are easily visible and identifiable in low tide. The isthmus which joins the eastern and western heads of Rainsford Island forms a semi-circular pattern creating a sheltered cove on the island's southern flank. Because of its nearness to the mainland, Rainsford is easily approached and one of the most frequently explored islands. During the summer, brightly-colored tents dot its meadow and shores. It is, perhaps, the favorite island in Boston Harbor for camping and picnicking.

This island was named in 1636 for its founder, Edward Raynsford, an Elder of the Old South Church in Boston. Later, the island was referred to as "Hospital Island" because of its quarantine hospitals. After Raynsford's death, many private individuals took possession of the island's rights in rapid succession until finally, in 1737, it was purchased by the City of Boston. A Quarantine Station and fever hospital were transferred to Rainsford Island from their previous location on Spectacle Island. Under the supervision of the City of Boston several buildings were erected. Among these were the "Greek Temple," the "Bowling Alleys," the "Old Mansion House," the "Superintendent's Quarters" and the "Dead House." The "Greek Temple," constructed in 1832 on the western head, was used as a smallpox hospital. It received its unusual name from the tall, white columns that decorated its entrance. This building provided a unique contrast to other buildings in Boston Harbor. A fever hospital was also located on the western bluff called "The Bowling Alleys," because of its long, rectangular shape.

On the great eastern head stood the "Old Mansion House," which had been built previous to the Quarantine Hospital in 1819. It was a summer resort hotel, perched on the summit of the hill, overlooking the scenic bay. In addition, the hospital superintendent's home and a morgue, or "Dead House," were also located on this bluff.

In the year 1852, the entire island was converted from a hospital into a pauper colony, where the poor folk of the City of Boston were given refuge. The women inhabited the structures located on the eastern bluff, while the men resided in those on the western head. At this time, a pier was constructed near the southern cove to service the boats that came to the island from the city. The remains of this pier can still be seen outlined in the water.

Eventually, the function of Rainsford Island as an almshouse location ceased, because this facility was moved to neighboring Long Island where it joined a chronic disease hospital. In its place, a boy's reform school was established that remained in existence for twenty-five years (from 1895–1920). However, by 1935 the buildings became vacated and in subsequent years, they were ravaged by fire and crumbled before the forces of the prevailing elements.

Rock Inscription—Rainsford Island

Rock Inscription—Rainsford Island

There is an unmarked graveyard situated on the western head of the island. Formerly, it was an ancient Indian burial ground, however, it became a resting place for the deceased inmates of the fever hospital, as well as for their keepers. Some of these graves have been excavated. Oddly enough, during the exhumation of one of these tombs, an iron sword-hilt was discovered, believed to have belonged to the Norseman Thorwald.[1] It is alleged that he once anchored in this harbor. Also, an interesting headstone was located there, but unfortunately no longer remains. It carried the inscription:

> "Nearby these grey rocks
> Enclosed in a box
> Lies Hatter Cox
> Who died of smallpox" [2]

This cemetery is all but smothered by weeds and is difficult to identify at present.

On the east side of the western bluff are several groups of rocks on which many curious inscriptions have been chiseled by former inhabitants and visitors to the island. One such inscription is said to be that of Edward Raynsford. Another states that "Dr. J. V. C. Smith was appointed physician for this island on June 14, 1826." He was the physician at the Quarantine Hospital, and later became the Mayor of Boston. Still another curious carving states that "Raynsford Isle was purchased for ye Indians, 1 pig, 2 pullets." Some of the stone markings are in Latin and Greek and in the form of advice or old proverbs. Others are merely names and dates. These stone carvings are one of the most interesting and intriguing features of this island.

Just beyond the west head, on "Quarantine Rocks," a fisherman known either as "Portuguese Joe," "Grisiano Rio" or "Joe the Rock," had built his home, perched high above the

---

[1] Sweetser, Moses Foster, *King's Handbook of Boston Harbor* (Cambridge, Mass.: Moses King Corp., 1882), p. 203.

[2] Snow, Edward Rowe, *Romance of Boston Bay* (Boston: Yankee Publishing Co., 1944), p. 151.

Rainsford Island

Greek Temple Ruins—Rainsford Island

water on iron stilts. However, it was destroyed by a fire in 1939.

Presently, Rainsford Island is owned by the City of Boston, and is used primarily for recreational purposes. The foundations of its past buildings are still discernible and can be easily identified by their locations. Exploration of Rainsford Island leaves one with a marked impression of peaceful serenity.

Quarantine Rocks—Rainsford Island

PEDDOCK'S ISLAND

Directly southwest of the Point Allerton Coast Guard Station in Hull, lies the private resort of Peddock's Island. This island is so situated that it completely separates the Harbors of Boston and Hingham. Comprised of four separate, though consecutive hills, joined by narrow spits of land, it looks like a giant sea-serpent reclining on the ocean floor, with parts of its body poking through the surface of the water.[1]

The northeastern hill, which constitutes the head of the serpent, is the largest of the island's four bluffs. On its slope, a number of massive, ivy-covered, brick buildings lie partially obscured by a thick growth of trees. All of these dwellings are presently deserted, however, during World Wars I and II, they served as quarters for military units stationed on Peddock's Island and later as homes for retired, non-commissioned officers. The interiors of the buildings are charred, their windows broken, and the wooden pillars at their entrances are rotting, eroded by the salt air. These edifices will eventually crumble, as most of the forsaken buildings on the other islands have, allowing the ravages of time to pick apart their walls, bit by bit. A maze of paved roads weave through the dense foliage. In many areas they are canopied by trees in such thickness that very little sunlight is able to reach their cracked and faded asphalt surface. Nestled neatly on the side of one of the roads, close to the southern beach, is a quaint, New England style church which gives the northeastern rise a warm and friendly aura.

On the middle of the island's three main hills are located

---

[1] Shurtleff, Nathaniel B., *Topographical and Historical Description of Boston* (Boston: Rockwell and Churchill, 1891), p. 440.

several small, summer cottages, not unlike those found in Hull or Nantasket. They are crowded together near the shore, inhabited only in the summer and abandoned during the winter.

The westernmost slope of Peddock's Island is heavily wooded similar to the northeastern embankment. It is a relatively uninhabited area except for some families living in the few small cottages that dot the landscape.

The tail of this imaginary serpent is the fourth hill which extends from the southwest portion of its body. It is a high, thin ridge of sand called "Prince's Head," named after Job Prince, a mariner in Boston waters during the seventeenth century.

The one hundred and thirteen acres of Peddock's Island received its name from Leonard Peddock, who was probably one of its first civilized inhabitants. Indians had thrived on this land before the Colonists settled in America. Around 1616, Frenchmen came to the island to trade goods with the Indians. They were ambushed and killed by the red men in a bloody massacre considered one of the worst in Boston's early history. The City of Charlestown took possession of the island in 1634, and allowed settlers to use its slopes for raising cattle and sheep. However, during the Revolution of 1775, British troops occupied Peddock's Island. Soldiers of the Continental Army raided the island and stole all of the livestock, thus leaving the British without food and forcing them to depart. The Continental forces then fortified the island in the event that the British should return.

England and France had been at war frequently since the mid-1600's and during the American Revolution the French aided the Colonists in an effort to undermine the British Empire. Consequently, vessels of the Royal Navy that prowled the waters of Boston Harbor after the war, trapped the battered French fleet of Count D'Estaing inside the harbor in 1778. To protect his ships, the Count erected crude defenses at the top of the northeastern bluff of Peddock's Island, as

Peddock's Island

well as on George's and Long Islands. These defensive measures forced the British fleet to retreat. The fortifications are no longer visible for they lie buried under heavy brush and sand. Later, in 1897, another fort was constructed, this time by the United States Government. This latter fort was called Fort Andrews, named after General Leonard Andrews who was a hero of the Civil War. During World War I, over two thousand army troops were stationed at Fort Andrews and quartered in the red brick dwellings that are scattered over the northeastern head of the island. A bleak reminder of its glorious past, this fort is barely recognizable now, resting beneath the overgrowth of shrubs and trees.

Peddock's Island was owned by private parties at various times throughout its history. Among these were the Cleverly family, in 1817, and the Jones family, in 1860.

Presently, this island is located in Plymouth County and is under the jurisdiction of the Metropolitan District Commission. A caretaker maintains the grounds and since it is an exclusively private island, it is accessible only to its summer inhabitants.

House of Worship—Peddock's Island

Military Quarters, Fort Andrews—Peddock's Island

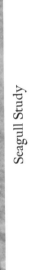

Seagull Study

HANGMAN'S ISLAND—SUNKEN LEDGE

Directly northwest of Peddock's Island lie two consecutive shoals. The first is merely a rocky bar infested with mussel beds and visible only at low tide. It is believed to have been a small island that has eroded away, hence its name Sunken Ledge. This bar is marked by a small granite pyramid at its northern point, which barely protrudes from the surface of the water at high tide. Just to the west of Sunken Ledge is another and larger, rugged rock formation called Hangman's Island. It is composed of granite and slate and capped by a small scrub area.

The origin of the name Hangman's Island is unknown, for pirates were never hung here as legend has stated. Hangman is probably a derivative of the island's original name, Hayman's Island which in turn probably originates from an early English immigrant. The land is accessible by way of a narrow, pebbly beach on the southern shore. The island once served as a home for fishermen, who lived in small, wooden shacks, and was used as a stone quarry. When Mrs. Olive Smallpiece purchased the island during the seventeenth century, she allowed its granite and slate rock to be quarried and taken to Boston where it was used as building material. Originally, the island is believed to have covered over an acre in area, but is now only one-quarter of an acre due to the removal of stone.

The last recorded owner of Hangman's Island was the Commonwealth of Massachusetts. Its present owner is unknown. Although it lies in Quincy Bay and within the limits of Norfolk County, the City of Quincy has never claimed it. Neither Sunken Ledge nor Hangman's Island serve any current purpose aside from being favorite fishing spots. To unsuspecting mariners, however, they can be a hazard.

Long Island Bridge from Moon to Long Island

LONG ISLAND

Long Island, named for its length, extends roughly one and three quarter miles out into the bay and, consisting of 216 acres, is the largest of the harbor islands. It lies directly east of Moon Island to which it is joined by a long steel bridge, built in 1951. This bridge spans the "Western Way" channel that divides these two islands, and links Long Island to the mainland. A Chronic Disease Hospital is perched atop the island's highest promontory. Its golden dome appears similar to that of Boston's State House, beautifully gilded and glistening in the bright sunlight. A tall red and white checkered water tower stands nearby, but somehow it seems out of place in this environment. In addition to the hospital, a deserted fortress and a small, white brick lighthouse are located on the northeastern point of the island. The fort, built to defend Boston Harbor, was active during the Civil and the two World Wars. The Long Island beacon was erected to warn mariners of the island's protruding northeasterly bluff.

Originally, Long Island was heavily wooded with trees; unfortunately, however, after plots of land were divided and sold to private parties by the Massachusetts Bay Colony in 1639, the new owners cut down most of the trees to provide room for farmland. One inhabitant, John Nelson, became well known for victoriously leading the colonists of Boston against the British troops under Sir Edmund Andros in the Battle of Fort Hill in 1689. Fort Hill, originally known as "Corn Hill," was located on the eastern side of Boston overlooking the bay. It acquired its name from a fortress that was built on its summit, in 1632. Andros was sent to America by King James II to govern the New England Colony. When he deprived the colonists of their democracy by overtaxing them, removing their charters and disallowing group assemblies, they revolted. This rebellion was one of the first in the New England Colony protesting British rule. Nelson captured Andros and imprisoned him at Castle Island; later, he was released and allowed to return to England. Ironically, Nelson himself was later captured at sea by the French and sent to Canada for confinement. Because he had learned of the French plans to raid the British colonies in America and had passed this information on to the English, he was deemed a spy, transported to France and imprisoned in the Paris Bastille. After his release in 1702, he returned to his island home in Boston Harbor, which at the time was still called "Nelson's Island." After his death the name was changed to Long Island, when the Long Island Company, in 1849, acquired the rights to it.

During the Revolutionary War of 1775, Long Island was occupied by the British. They were forced to evacuate the island when continental troops landed and stole their livestock, leaving them without food. Following the British evacuation of the City of Boston in March of 1776, the Continental Army constructed crude defenses on Long Island's eastern bluff to protect the City from the British Fleet which lingered in the harbor. These defensive measures, coupled with those on the other islands, eventually drove the British away, although, when the War of 1812 broke out, the British Fleet returned and again prowled the waters of Boston Harbor. In 1814, they blockaded the frigate "U.S.S. Constitution" just off Long Island's northeastern shore. One year later the Constitution was able to escape into safe and open waters by sailing through Shirley Gut, which lay between Winthrop and Deer Island.[1]

---

[1] Snow, Edward Rowe, *Sailing Down Boston Bay* (Boston: Boston Printing Co., 1941), p. 25.
(This waterway is filled in today, linking Deer Island to the mainland.)

Long Island Hospital

When the Long Island Company purchased the island in 1849, the "Long Island House" and the "Long Island Hotel" were built with the intention of developing a summer resort area. However, with the onset of the Civil War, Union troops were stationed at Camp Wrightman on Long Island and were quartered in these residences. The Fourth Regiment, encamped here, eventually became the first northern force to invade Confederate Virginia. In 1865, Fort Strong, named in honor of Governor Caleb Strong, was constructed on the northeastern promontory of Long Island. Previously, it had been located on the now extinct Noddle's Island in East Boston. Fort Strong was used not only during the Civil War, but also, in both World Wars.

Throughout the mid-1800's, Portuguese fishing families lived in crude shacks on the island's shores, but they were eventually evicted after the City of Boston took possession of the island in 1882. When the City Almshouse was closed on Rainsford Island in the latter 1800's, another one was built on Long Island together with a Chronic Disease Hospital. The Almshouse and Hospital were serviced by ferries from the mainland until the bridge was erected. The lighthouse, originally constructed on the northeastern slope in 1819, was relocated on the other side of the same slope in 1898. Presently, it stands one hundred and twenty feet high, operates automatically, and shines continuously for a distance of fifteen to seventeen miles.

The Long Island Hospital is currently managed by the Department of Health and Hospitals of the City of Boston in association with the Boston City and Mattapan Hospitals. Although Fort Strong is deserted, its massive cement walls serve as a reminder of its glorious history. Long Island stands proudly in the harbor, an asset to the community, performing its important functions.

Long Island Light

Birch Trees—Moon Island

MOON ISLAND

Although still referred to as an island, Moon Island is really a peninsula that extends eastward from Squantum. It is located in Norfolk County and is used as a training center for firemen, a police target range and as the site of open sewerage vats. Despite these schools and somewhat offensive vats, however, it is still a unique and beautiful island. Its forty-four acres gradually ascend from the west to a high bluff on the eastern side, from which most of the harbor can be seen. The summit of this hill is crowded with scrub bushes, most of which are wild bayberry that shelter an abundance of pheasant and quail. In early winter, the clusters of bayberries appear as tiny, blue lights against a gray sky. On the western side of the slope there is also a grove of tall birch trees, a rarity on the islands. Wandering through this grove one almost feels as if he is strolling in the woods of Maine or Vermont, instead of on an island in Boston Harbor.

Originally, Moon Island was known as "Manning's" or "Mennen's Moone," probably named for an early English immigrant. Its first recorded owner was John Holland, in 1665. The City of Boston acquired the island in 1878 and constructed sewerage vats to service parts of Quincy and Boston. These vats were made of granite that came from quarries in Quincy and Cape Ann. At the same time, a causeway was built to link Moon Island with Squantum and to conceal the pipes leading to the vats. This road was constructed of sand and gravel taken from "Half Moon Island," a crescent-shaped land mass, located at the mouth of Black's Creek in Quincy Bay. After the removal of its earth, all that remained of Half Moon was a vast expanse of mussel beds visible only in low tide. Later, in 1892, a garbage reclaiming plant was erected on Moon Island, but it was subsequently moved to neighboring Spectacle Island in 1912.

The sewerage vats are still in use, servicing the community of Squantum but are to be discontinued in the near future. The waste will be pumped instead to a disposal facility on Nut Island in Hough's Neck. Although it has never acquired much of an historical background, Moon Island serves a practical purpose with its training centers, and is a popular fishing area as well.

The island has a great deal of natural beauty that unfortunately, has been obscured; its charm, however, still attracts an occasional explorer.

Open Sewerage Vats—Moon Island

Field of Queen Anne's Lace—Spectacle Island

SPECTACLE ISLAND

Spectacle Island is comprised of two large circular hills joined together by a narrow isthmus. Consequently, its name was derived from its shape, which closely resembles a pair of eyeglasses, or spectacles. The two hills constitute the lenses of the spectacles while the connecting isthmus represents the bridge. This island, however, could well have been named "The Isle of Beauty," because most of its ninety-seven acres is covered with lush vegetation. Wild rose bushes swarming with locust-sized queen bees, and fleecy-white discs of Queen Anne's Lace dot its almost impenetrable slopes. Head-high shrubs squeeze wildly among the grasses and underbrush forming an entanglement of roots and vines too thick to walk through.

The shoreline of this island displays a dazzling assortment of articles swept in by the waves. Multicolored, crystal-like, beachglass, polished by the surf and glazed by the sun, lies strewn among pock-marked morsels of sandstone and red brick. Oddly, there are also a numerous variety of colored marbles and unusual objects that look like doorknobs. Interwoven through all of this are delicate webs of soft, dark-green, mermaid's-hair seaweed. A musical sound, similar to that made by chimes dangling in the wind, can be heard all along the beach. It is caused by waves from passing motorboats that wash the beach-glass gently back and forth upon the rocks, creating a high-pitched, symphonic echo.

Unfortunately, the natural beauty of this charming island has been tainted by its unsavory history. After the Bill family gave up posession of Spectacle in 1742, a rendering plant, a garbage reclaiming plant, a disposal company, and a ravaging fire destroyed all that nature herself could not protect.

In 1684, Samuel Bill bought Spectacle Island from Josiah, son of Wampatuck, the chief of the Massachusetts Indians. The City of Boston purchased the land from Bill in 1717 and erected a Quarantine Station to treat those persons coming into port on foreign vessels, who were suffering with infectious diseases. However, shortly after its completion, the Quarantine Station was relocated on Rainsford Island. The Bill family then reacquired the rights to the island in 1739 only to sell them again in 1742. Until this time, it was not uncommon to observe bears and other wild animals roaming the land's hummocks, and to see hay and garden vegetables covering a portion of its soil. In the early part of the 1800's, two summer resort hotels were built on the island but were forced to close shortly after opening because of illegal gambling carried on there. Later, in 1857, Nahum Ward opened a rendering factory on Spectacle. All of Boston's deceased horses were transported across the bay to this factory where they were processed into tallow, suet, hair, hides and oil.

In 1912, a garbage reclaiming plant that had previously been located on Moon Island, was moved to Spectacle's shores. It was owned and operated by the Boston Development and Sanitary Company, who sold it to the Coleman Disposal Company in 1922. Its industrial waste slowly buried a section of the island, covering it with heaping mounds of rubbish and debris. These waste piles are of such magnitude that they have filled in the indentation of the connecting isthmus, and have obscured the island's original configuration.

Range lights were constructed on Spectacle's northern bluff in 1932, but were destroyed by a severe fire in 1934. This blaze enveloped the entire northern slope, destroying most of the buildings on the island.

At present the island is located in Suffolk County and is multiply owned. The City of Boston owns one-half of the land, one quarter is privately owned, and the remaining quarter is divided between the Boston Edison Company and the

Reclaiming Plant—Spectacle Island

East Coast Realty Corporation. The northern bluff is still bleak and savagely charred, a grim reminder of the 1934 fire. However, a beachcomber walking along the southern bluff and its beaches will be captivated by its charm if he disregards the island's unsavory past. The wild vegetation will catch even the most unalert and salt-weary eye.

View of Spectacle Island from Moon Island

THOMPSON'S ISLAND

Thompson's Island, located in Suffolk County is 157 acres of rolling hills, vast meadows and long beaches. It is located just northwest of Moon Island and is the only land mass in Boston Harbor between the residential community of Squantum and the City of Boston. Plowed fields of golden hay span its gentle slopes. A large, shallow cove choked by stalks of eel-grass, and partially filled by a maze of pebbly sandbars, is located on the island's western side. This cove was at one time much larger, but was damned and diked sometime during the mid-1800's, so that the inhabitants of the island could use the water to irrigate their fields. As a result, a vast meadow now fills in part of what was once the cove itself, and at this site, the first trading post in all of Boston Harbor was established by David Thompson. Protruding from the western bank and running in a southerly direction, lies a sandbar that stretches almost as far as Squantum in low tide, save for a narrow channel that separates the two land masses. This bar was noted by the early Puritans for its abundance of clams. A large well-built wharf located on the northwestern shore of the island is used by boats that ferry back and forth from South Boston.

The first inhabitants of Thompson's Island were the Indians who maintained campsites on most of the harbor islands. David Thompson, a Scotsman, came to Boston Harbor in 1619, for the purpose of setting up a trading post to barter with the Indians. He chose Thompson's Island because of its large, sheltered cove, and the island's proximity to the mainland. Shortly thereafter, Thompson had to return to England. Upon his arrival in Britain, he made arrangements with William Trevour and Captain Miles Standish, who were about to embark on the Mayflower, to claim this island for him. After their arrival in New England, on an excursion into Boston Harbor from the Plimoth Bay Colony in 1621, William Trevour claimed this land for Thompson but called it "Island of Trevour."

Thompson, who was employed in England as Agent and Attorney for the "Council for New England," came to America in 1623 to colonize the region known today as northern New England. He landed at "Little Harbor," located at the mouth of the Piscataqua River and called his plantation "Pannaway," the original Indian name for this land. Today, this site is known as Odiornes Point in Rye, New Hampshire. At this settlement, Thompson constructed a fort for protection against the Indians, a blacksmith shop and a trading post. However, it wasn't until 1626 that he left the New Hampshire Colony and sailed into Boston Harbor to finally claim the island that had been granted to him by Trevour. He changed its name to "Thompson's Island" and established what is believed to be the first permanent settlement by a colonist in Boston Harbor. Thompson had a variety of occupations such as fishing, trading, hunting and farming. Unfortunately, he died only two years after moving there.

After Thompson's death the Massachusetts Bay Colony took possession of the island and later, in 1634, granted it to the Town of Dorchester. In 1648, Thompson's son John claimed the island as his legal inheritance. However, he forfeited his rights to the land six years later because of indebtedness to some Bristol County merchants. In 1666, the Lynde family purchased the island and owned it for 148 years, using the land solely for farming.

During the American Revolution of 1775, the British seized Thompson's Island, along with several other Boston islands. They were forced to evacuate, however, when Con-

Thompson's Island in Winter

tinental troops set the island on fire. The last private owner
of the island was George W. Beale who sold it to the trustees
of the "Boston Farm School" in 1834. At this time, the island
was annexed to the City of Boston. The school was united
with the "Boston Asylum for Indigent Boys" and in 1835,
a new schoolhouse was erected on the island called the "Farm
and Trades School." Originally, the purpose of the school
was to house homeless orphans and teach them practical farming and mechanical trades. At present, it is a private, prepara-
tory school called "Thompson's Academy" which educates
boys from the 9th through 12th grades.

This island, like others in the harbor, has been the site
of several unfortunate incidents. One mishap occurred in
1842, when a boat containing several students and a teacher
capsized during a sudden squall. Twenty-three boys and the
instructor were drowned. Several years later, in 1892, a
helium balloon that had taken off from the Boston Common,
crashed just off the shore of the island killing the pilot and
one crew member.

In 1846, Theodore Lyman, a former superintendent of the
school, donated and planted a grove of approximately 6,000
trees on the southwestern slope, replacing those that were
burned during the Revolutionary War. Appropriately, it is
called "Lyman's Grove." Of historic significance is the fact
that the first high school band in America was organized at
the school in 1857 under the direction of John Morse.

Thompson's Island is located within the boundaries of Suffolk County. Currently, in addition to classrooms, Thompson's Academy has football, baseball, track, tennis and bad-
minton facilities, as well as a gymnasium and several dormi-
tories. Just recently, however, during the winter of 1971, a
fire destroyed the old Administration building. Among some
of the well-known graduates from Thompson's Academy are
Clarence DeMar, a famous marathon runner and "Big Brother"

Cove on Thompson's Island

Bob Emery, of radio and television fame. The school stands as a tribute to its boys who have served in challenging and diversified careers. David Thompson's island trading post has undergone many changes, and the Academy continues to serve a meaningful purpose, for the advancement of mankind.

Thompson's Academy

CASTLE ISLAND

Fortifications have been erected on most of the islands in Boston Harbor. However, the two fortresses that stand foremost are Fort Warren on George's Island, built to protect the entrance to the harbor, and Fort Independence on Castle Island, constructed to protect both the inner harbor and the City of Boston.

Castle Island, located in South Boston, is actually no longer an island since it is now connected to the mainland by an artificial causeway. Its monumental fortress is easily accessible but the interior of the fort has been closed to sightseers. Since the construction of the causeway, Castle's Island's twenty acres have become a highly commercialized picnic and fishing area as well as a popular tourist attraction.

The island was first settled in 1634 by the Puritans under the leadership of Thomas Dudley, Governor of the Massachusetts Bay Colony. The Puritans chose this location because of its proximity to the mainland. In 1635, crude defenses were erected to protect their other settlements from the French, who had destroyed an English trading post near the Kennebec River in Maine. The fort, originally built of pine logs fastened together with mud, was later reconstructed with stone, the finished product resembling a castle: hence its name, "Castle Island." It was one of the first fortresses constructed in the Boston area and was also the first fort in the United States to remain in continuous use until the conclusion of the Spanish-American War. During most of the 1600's both the island and fort were run by the colonists under the supervision of the British government. However, in a minor rebellion in 1689, John Nelson, of Long Island, led a group of Bostonians against the British in the "Battle of Fort Hill." Sir Edmund Andros, Governor of the New England Colony and leader of the British forces, was captured and imprisoned at Castle Island. (See pages 71–72.)

Various other skirmishes occurred between American colonists and English loyalists that eventually resulted in the Revolution of 1775. At the start of the Colonial rebellion, the British commanded the fort on Castle Island, which at that time was called "Castle William" in honor of a former king of England. For a short interval, the fort's guns fired on the Continental forces entrenched at Dorchester Heights, now part of South Boston. Near the conclusion of the war, in March of 1776, the British evacuated the port of Boston and in the process of fleeing from the harbor, destroyed Castle William. General George Washington ordered the fort rebuilt after the war and Paul Revere, the renowned "nightrider," was placed in charge of the reconstruction operations. In 1779, John Hancock, President of the Continental Congress and the first to sign the Declaration of Independence, was placed in command of the new fort. After Hancock was relieved of his command in 1781, Fort Independence functioned as a prison. It was the first state penitentiary in Massachusetts and later, in 1799 President John Adams changed its name from "Castle William" to "Fort Independence."

An incident occurred on Castle Island that became immortalized in American literature. In 1817, a twenty-one-year-old Lieutenant, Robert F. Massie of Virginia, was killed by one Captain Green during a sword duel on the island. Lieutenant Massie was buried where he fell and the grave was marked by a marble monument. To avenge his death, fellow soldiers sealed Massie's murderer in a dungeon of the fort and left him to die. Later, in 1827, a famous author, Edgar Allen Poe enlisted in the United States Army and was stationed at the island fortress under the assumed name of Edgar A. Perry.[1] His book, *The Cask of Amontillado* was based upon this

---

[1] Snow, Edward Rowe, *Romance of Boston Bay* (Boston, Yankee Publishing Co., 1944), p. 68.

Fort Independence—Castle Island

duel and the subsequent entombment of Captain Green. Massie's grave is no longer at Castle Island, but has been relocated at Fort Devens, Massachusetts. Because his remains were moved so often, first from Castle Island to Governor's Island, and then to Deer Island, before finally resting at Fort Devens, he has been called "The Roving Skeleton of Boston Harbor." [2]

In 1833, Fort Independence underwent another reconstruction under the direction of Lieutenant Sylvanus Thayer, who had been a long-term superintendent at West Point Military Academy. Simultaneously, he was also placed in charge of renovating Fort Warren on George's Island. Therefore, Fort Independence on Castle Island and Fort Warren on George's Island have similar dimensions and are sometimes referred to as "The Twin Forts." In 1879, Fort Independence was decommissioned and the troops stationed there were moved to George's Island. During the Spanish-American War of 1898, the fort was used as a mine and torpedo station, and later in 1911 as a summer school for the sick children of South Boston which remained in use for several years. In 1925, an artificial causeway was constructed linking Castle Island to the mainland, making the newly-formed peninsula a favorite site for tourists and visitors.

Today, Castle Island, like George's Island, is operated by the Metropolitan District Commission and is highly developed for public recreation. A large, obelisk monument, erected in memory of Donald McKay, a famous shipbuilder of East Boston, stands fifty-two feet high on the island's eastern bank. During the mid-1800's, McKay built the famous clipper ship "Flying Cloud," that broke the sailing vessel record from Boston to San Francisco.

Castle Island, with its fort, is located in Suffolk County and is one of the most historic landmarks in Boston. Combined with Fort Warren on George's Island, it has made Boston Harbor one of the best protected seaports in the United States.

---

[2] Snow, Edward Rowe, *Sailing Down Boston Bay* (Boston: Boston Printing Co., 1941), p. 16.

Entrance to Fort Independence—Castle Island

McKay Monument—Castle Island

BOSTON LIGHT—LITTLE BREWSTER ISLAND

Boston Light is located on Little Brewster Island, at the entrance to Boston Harbor. It was North America's first lighthouse and is one of the most picturesque beacons in the entire world.

Before Boston Light was erected, a small range-light stood on the summit of the huge bluff on Great Brewster Island. However, as trade and commerce increased in the port of Boston, there arose a need for a more powerful beacon to guide the incoming ships safely past "Shag Rocks" that loom to the east of Little Brewster Island. Consequently, the light was erected on Little Brewster in 1716. Since then, this island has often been referred to as "Beacon Island" or "Lighthouse Island." The first of its many keepers was George Worthylake, who served two years and then drowned at sea when his dory capsized while he was returning to the light from the mainland. His wife and daughter also perished during this incident.

Boston Light has played a most significant role in Boston's history. In the early 1700's, the keeper at the light would signal Castle Island of approaching enemy vessels by raising the Union Jack flag. The raised flag would warn the City and give its citizens and militia ample time to prepare their defenses.[1] During the American Revolution of 1775, the British forces captured the light and blocked the entrance to the harbor. In an unsuccessful attempt to drive the British off Little Brewster Island, Major Vose landed with Continental troops and succeeded in partially destroying the beacon. A

---

[1] Sweetser, Moses Foster, *King's Handbook of Boston Harbor* (Cambridge, Mass.: Moses King Corp., 1882), p. 246.

few days later, Major Tupper, in command of three hundred Continentals, was dispatched by General George Washington to put the light out of commission permanently. They succeeded in their mission, but suffered heavy casualties when their boats were stranded by the outgoing tide. They were closely pursued by the enemy until batteries on Nantasket Head heavily damaged the British craft. As a grand finale to this episode, the British completely destroyed the light subsequent to their evacuation of the City of Boston in March, 1776. Because of its strategic importance, Boston Light was restored by the Massachusetts Legislature in 1783. This latest beacon still stands today, although it has been remodelled several times. It is built of granite, one hundred and three feet high and shines sixteen miles out to sea, flashing at ten second intervals. In 1790, the United States Government took possession of Little Brewster Island and Boston Light.

During the War of 1812, the British fleet returned once more to Boston Harbor and in 1813, just off the shores of Little Brewster, a famous naval battle took place between the American frigate "Chesapeake" and the British vessel "Shannon." Although the "Shannon" emerged victorious, it was during this skirmish that Captain James Lawrence of the "Chesapeake" shouted his famous command, "Don't give up the ship," which has since become a much-used battle-cry.

In 1844, a cigar factory was established on Little Brewster Island, and Bostonians actually believed that the cigars manufactured here were imported from Spain. This devious venture, however, was terminated after a short time.

During World War II the beacon was extinguished as a safety precaution, and was relit after the War.

Today Boston Light stands as a monument, commemorating incidents of both the Revolutionary War and the War of 1812. Its bright beacon, supplemented by a fog horn, guides vessels into the historic and friendly seaport of Boston.

Boston Light—Little Brewster Island

Graves Light

GRAVES LIGHT

The outermost light in Boston Harbor is Graves Light, located five miles east of Winthrop and about one and one-half miles northeast of the Brewster Islands. It is a gray, granite structure, the lone sentry at the entrance to the "North" ship channel. This beacon was erected on ten acres of jagged rocks and ledges that have caused many tragic shipwrecks. The name of the light was derived from one of two sources. It is possible that these shoals were named after Thomas Graves, the Vice-Admiral of John Winthrop's fleet, as well as the first foreign trader out of America. However, due to the numerous shipwrecks and the many lives that were lost at this location, it has been said that the pointed rocks look like headstones marking the watery graves of the drowned, hence the term "The Graves."

Graves Light was built in 1903 and stands ninety-eight feet high. Its beacon flashes sixteen miles out to sea, twice every six seconds. It is still actively manned by a keeper, although even after it was erected many ships still foundered there. The ship *City of Salisbury*, carrying a cargo of wild animals, struck a submerged portion of the perilous ledge in 1938 and sank, losing much of its cargo. Shortly thereafter, in 1941, during a winter gale, the *Mary E. O'Hara*, a fishing boat, hit "Finn's Ledge" just to the west of the light. It is reported that the crew survived for as long as they could, clinging to the masts swaying above the water until their hands froze, and they dropped to their deaths in the cold, turbulent sea.[1] Only a few crewmen survived this disaster.

---

[1] Snow, Edward Rowe, *Sailing Down Boston Bay* (Boston: Boston Printing Co., 1941), p. 39.

These are only two of the countless wrecks that have occurred on these dreadful and treacherous shoals.

Today, Graves Light is a sentinel, cautioning vessels and warning of the rocks that must be avoided for a safe entry into Boston Harbor from the northeast.

MINOT'S LEDGE LIGHT

The "Cohasset Rocks" are a vast series of dangerous rocks and ledges located just off the coast of Cohasset, Massachusetts. Most of these shoals are submerged at high tide and unmarked, causing many shipwrecks. The easternmost shoal, located approximately three miles southeast of Nantasket Beach, is called Minot's Ledge. This underwater cliff has accounted for more wrecks and deaths than any other one hazardous area in and around Boston Harbor.

Minot's Ledge is said to have been named for George Minot of Dorchester, who was a merchant in Boston. Allegedly, he lost one of his vessels on this shoal around 1754. His family was also notorious for smuggling gunpowder to the Bostonians during the Revolution of 1775.

Minot's Ledge barely emerges at low tide, and becomes dangerously submerged when the tide rises. Due to the countless wrecks that occurred here, a light tower was erected in 1850, to warn mariners of the imminent danger. This tower consisted of a beacon and living quarters perched on top of nine iron stilts drilled into the rock. Just a year after its completion, the two keepers, Joseph Wilson, an Englishman, and Joseph Antoine, a Portuguese, were killed when the structure collapsed during a severe storm. Waves reaching one hundred feet in height were recorded during the storm.[1] The ledge was marked by a lightship until 1860, when the present lighthouse was completed. This edifice stands ninety-seven feet high and is solidly constructed of granite quarried from the City of Quincy and from Government Island in Cohas-

---

[1] Snow, Edward Rowe, *Sailing Down Boston Bay* (Boston: Boston Printing Co., 1941), p. 53.

set.[2] In 1894, the sequence of flashes from its beacon was changed to one-four-three—popularly interpreted as "I Love You." Consequently, it has sometimes been referred to as the "Lover's Light."

Since the present lighthouse was constructed, few ships have foundered on Minot's Ledge. Currently automatic, the beacon's fifteen-mile radius complements Boston Light, Graves Light and the Lightship making Boston Harbor safe for travel and commerce.

Minot's Light

[2] Coast Guard, U.S., *Historically Famous Lighthouses* (Washington, D.C.: Public Information Division, 1957), p. 44.

BOSTON LIGHTSHIP

The once treacherous waters of Boston Harbor have become among the safest in America in the course of the last century. The entrance to the harbor is marked by what is commonly known as "The four cornered safety square," [1] formed by Graves Light to the north, Minot's Light to the south, Boston Light to the west and the Boston Lightship to the east.

The Boston Lightship is a large, bulky vessel, anchored approximately five miles east of Nantasket Beach. Two light towers rise from its deck, fifty-three feet above the water, providing a guiding beam with a thirteen-mile radius. Written in bold, white letters on its bright, red hull is the word "BOSTON," greeting foreign vessels on their arrival at this friendly port.

The first lightship anchored here in 1894 was rammed on two occasions by incoming vessels that were driven off course during storms. When forced to go into drydock for repairs, the lightship is temporarily replaced by a similar craft, called the "Relief" Ship.

The Boston Lightship completes the safety precautions taken by the Coast Guard and other Marine associations to protect inbound ships from the harbor's hazards.

---

[1] Snow, Edward Rowe, *Romance of Boston Bay* (Boston: Yankee Publishing Co., 1944), p. 294.

Brewster Spit

BREWSTER SPIT—BUG LIGHT

The "Great Brewster Spit" is a hazard to navigators in Boston Harbor. It is a low-level, rocky bar that runs from the southwestern shore of Great Brewster Island to within a few hundred yards of George's Island. Visible only at low tide, it loops like a snake across the water and is bordered on either side by dense beds of kelp seaweed, whose slimy, rubber-like fans sway in the current beneath the water's surface. Directly south of the spit lies a circular hill of pebbly sand called "False Spit." At low tide, it is crowded with seagulls; it is submerged, however, when the water rises.

A small beacon was erected at the western extremity of Great Brewster Spit in 1856, consisting of living quarters and a lantern perched thirty-five feet above the gravel on seven iron poles. It is from these spindly, insect-like legs, still standing today, that the structure received its name, "Bug Light." It is also referred to as "Spit Light." The purpose of Bug Light in addition to marking the end of the spit, was to guide incoming vessels clear of Harding's Ledge, which is located two miles east of Point Allerton. This was accomplished by aligning Bug Light with the lighthouse on Long Island, thus setting a safe, unhindered course. Mr. Turner, the "King of Calf Island," was the light's first keeper, and was succeeded by others, until the wooden structure burned in 1929. After the fire, an automatic beacon and bell were placed on top of the original spindly-legged base.

Presently, Bug Light marks the southeastern boundary and Lovell's Island, the northwestern boundary of the "Black Rock Channel." This waterway runs northeastward from the Narrows Channel and is used mainly by pleasure craft.

Bug Light

DEER ISLAND LIGHT

Deer Island Light is a strange, primeval-looking structure located approximately five hundred yards southwest of Deer Island in Winthrop. Its stocky shape and reddish-brown color provide a striking contrast to the harbor's other sleek and streamlined beacons. It is built of granite and cement, encircled by four tiers of catwalks. Standing fifty-three feet high, its light flashes a distance of fifteen miles out into the harbor.

Constructed in 1890, Deer Island Light marks a small, treacherous sandbar called "Fawn Bar." It is located within the "President Roads" shipping channel, the main waterway within the harbor. Just to the east of the light is a small pile of granite rocks, placed there to break the force of the waves that buffet the beacon. The first of the many keepers of Deer Island Light was Wesley Pingree. Others were Judson and Tom Small, and Joseph McCabe, who drowned in the winter of 1916 while walking on melting ice near the light.

Deer Island Light is still manned by a keeper. This structure and the nearby tower of Nix's Mate present a most unusual and dramatic appearance in the inner part of Boston Harbor.

Deer Island Light

GUIDE TO THE CHANNELS

Large Channels

The *Main Ship Channel* runs between Boston and East Boston, from the Mystic River to the "Presidents Roads Channel." Along its banks are located the wharves and piers that accommodate vessels from all parts of the world. It is suited for large craft and averages sixty feet in low tide.

The *Presidents Roads Channel* runs eastward from the "Main Ship Channel," between Long Island and Winthrop. Its original name was "King's Road" and, also suited for large vessels, it averages forty-five feet in low tide.

The *Broad Sound Channel* or

The *Modern Ship Channel* extends northeastward from the "President Roads" into the open sea. Suited for large vessels, it averages sixty feet at low tide.

The *Nantasket Roads Channel* runs east to west between Boston Light and Pt. Allerton in Hull. Originally called "Ship Channel," it is suited for large vessels, and averages sixty feet in low tide.

The *Narrows Channel* connects the "President Roads" with the "Nantasket Roads" Channel, running from northwest to southeast between Gallop's and Lovell's Islands. Its original name was the "Old Main Channel" and it is suited for medium and large-sized vessels. It averages thirty feet in low tide.

111

The *Black Rock Channel* runs northeast to southwest between Lovell's Island and Bug Light, joining the "Narrows Channel" to the "Hypocrite Channel." It is suited for medium-sized craft and averages twenty-five feet in low tide.

Small Channels

The *Nubble Channel* runs southward from the "President Roads," between Long and Gallop's Islands, to the "Nantasket Roads." It is suited for smaller craft and averages fifteen feet in low tide.

The *Hypocrite Channel* runs northeast to southwest between Green and Little Calf Islands, and joins to the "Black Rock Channel." Although it averages seventy feet at low tide, it is used only by small boats because of Aldridge, Devils' Back and Half-Tide Ledges located at its western end.

The *Hull Gut Channel* extends from "Nantasket Roads" southward, between the Pt. Allerton Coast Guard Station and Peddock's Island, into Hingham Bay. It is used by large craft approaching the Fore River Shipyard and averages thirty-five feet at low tide.

West Gut is the channel running between Peddock's and Nut Islands into Hingham Bay. Suited only for small boats, it averages twenty-five feet at low tide.

The *Western Way Channel* extends southward from "President Roads," under the Long Island Bridge and into Quincy Bay. It is used only by small boats and averages ten feet at low tide.

Sheltered Seagull Nest

Vacated Resting Place

GUIDE TO THE ROCKS AND LEDGES

The Outer Harbor

Harding's Ledge, located two miles east of Pt. Allerton in Hull was originally called "Conney Hasset Rock," the Indian name for Cohasset. The ledge, submerged in high tide and emerging four feet above the water in low tide, is marked by a bell buoy. It has been the site of several shipwrecks.

Shag Rocks, originally called "Egg Rocks" because of the shape of the largest boulder in this group, are located just to the east of Little Brewster Island. They always protrude from the water's surface and have been the cause of several shipwrecks. Two noted wrecks were the "Maritana" in 1861 in which many lives were lost, and the "Fanny Pike" in 1882, wherein the crew was rescued.

Martin Ledge and Boston Ledge are located to the east of Outer Brewster Island. They are permanently submerged, approximately fourteen feet below the surface in low tide, and are marked by buoys.

Aldridge Ledge, Devils' Back and Half-Tide Rocks are three sets of ledges located directly southwest of Green Island. Aldridge lies submerged three feet below the surface in low tide, Devils' Back one foot below, and Half-Tide uncovers four feet in low water. Of the three only Half-Tide is marked by a buoy since it lies within the Hypocrite Channel.

Roaring Bulls, Maffit Ledge and *Commissioner's Ledge* are three sets of rocks which present dangerous unmarked hazards in a waterway that is sometimes mistaken for a channel located between Graves Light and Green Island. The Roaring Bulls are located directly southwest of Graves Light and emerge eight feet in low tide. Maffit and Commissioner's Ledges lie to the north of Green Island and both are permanently submerged.

Split Rock and *Round Rock* lie between Great and Middle Brewster Islands. They received their names from their shapes. Each uncovers at low tide and both are unmarked.

Pope Rock is located just east of Calf Island. It is unmarked.

Toddy Rocks are located just north of Hull near the "Nantasket Roads Channel." They are unmarked, sitting three feet below the water's surface in low tide.

Centurion Rock is located directly southeast of George's Island. It is a large boulder, originally called "Saint Turens Rock," that uncovers in low tide and is unmarked.

Black Rocks are a pile of rocks on the northwestern bank of the Brewster Spit. They received their name from their dark color. They are unmarked and are visible only in low tide.

The Inner Harbor

Hospital Shoal is a vast expanse of rock-ridden mudflats located northeast of Rainsford Island. This stretch is usually submerged except in the lowest tide of a full moon.

Quarantine Rocks, located southwest of Rainsford Island, are so named because of the Quarantine Hospitals that once stood on the island. They consist of four sets of unmarked ledges, that are visible in low tide. Only the set nearest the island remains visible at high tide.

Camel Rock, shaped like the hump on a camel's back, is an unmarked boulder located just northeast of Long Island. It becomes visible at low tide.

Sculpin Ledge is a kelp-infested bar that uncovers in low tide and is located to the south of Spectacle Island. It is unmarked.

Thimble Island is a pile of rocks continuously above water, located to the west of Thompson's Island. It has sometimes been called "Rat Island."

A Final Note

Since this book was written, proposals for the development of the islands have become somewhat of a reality. On November 17, 1972, Governor Francis W. Sargent announced that an agreement had been reached for the State to purchase Great Brewster Island, where the establishment of nature trails and primitive campsites are planned. The State is also planning to acquire other islands before further changes, as set down by the Metropolitan Area Planning Council, are carried out.

EPILOGUE

"The Boston Harbor Islands are a rare combination of land and water resource—a resource that has a uniqueness not available in our parks and land preserves." This statement was made by Senator Edward M. Kennedy in his article, "A New Future for the Islands in Boston Harbor," which appeared in the July, 1972 edition of *Yankee Magazine*. It sums up Senator Kennedy's feelings that Boston Harbor and its islands should be cleaned and preserved as a parkland and recreation area. His view is shared by everyone who is familiar with the islands.

It is unfortunate that several of the islands contain unnecessary trash and debris deposited by careless, unconcerned sightseers and campers. However, the romance and natural beauty of Boston Harbor still remains. This is a wild, untamed land, exploding with all of the wonders of nature. The rugged rock formations, molded by endless pounding from the roaring surf, the scrubby vegetation that blooms in all of its radiant glory during spring and mid-summer, and the deserted beaches cluttered with strange artifacts from the sea, all dazzle the adventurer with their united majesty. Where else can one find acres upon acres of delicate Queen Anne's Lace swaying gently in cool, easterly breezes, and then, a few paces closer to the shore, clusters of white daisies, bayberry, wild roses and morning glory, all fighting for supremacy. On the beach of any one of the islands, one may find a rich assortment of driftwood and other seaswept items, not to mention the abundant marine life. Red, brown and green algae, boulders covered with barnacles and periwinkles, and an occasional starfish or fiddler crab inhabit this region of no-mans-land that separates the briny deep from the exposed hills and valleys. It is where the land meets the sea. The struggle is eternal and the ocean seems to reign.

Aside from the ecology of the islands, Boston Harbor is an historic seaport. Its background dates from the time of the Norsemen, to the Puritans, through the Indian, Revolutionary, Civil and Spanish-American Wars, and up through the World Wars to the present. Boston Light was the first lighthouse in all of North America. Fort Independence and Fort Warren are two of the finest constructed fortresses in the United States. As a matter of fact, Boston Harbor has been one of the most defensible and best protected seaports in this country over the centuries. The story of Lovers Rock, curious inscriptions carved into slate, and the legend of the Lady in Black all lend a touch of romance and mystery to the islands. Toppled buildings of a bygone era and overgrown foundations of inns, resorts, hospitals, factories and private homes bring the harbor's past back into focus. These islands represent the heart and soul of New England, its past life-style and the hearty and courageous people who settled here. Exploring each island will excite the nostalgia that inevitably lingers deep in every soul. What other part of the country represents some 350 plus years of United States history?

Despite all of this acclaim, Boston Harbor and its islands is a relatively undiscovered paradise. The main reason for this is the inaccessibility and isolation of the islands. Several million people live within a short drive of the Boston waterfront, but few realize the historical significance of the harbor, let alone the untamed beauty that awaits the adventurer beyond the crowded shoreline of the mainland. It has been estimated that over 100,000 people visit George's Island and Fort Warren each year, and several thousand more journey to historic Castle Island in South Boston. However, the remaining land is still an undiscovered wilderness, especially to the present generation. Boston Harbor is approximately fifty square miles in area containing about one hundred eighty miles of shoreline and roughly

three hundred acres of land on thirty islands. It seems a shame that this beautiful land, once a flourishing community outside of Boston should go unheralded as it is at present.

There have been many varied proposals for the redevelopment of the islands. For instance, Long, Moon and Spectacle Islands, serviced by Ferries from Boston or South Boston, could be used for swimming, picnicking, fishing or just leisurely walking. There has been a proposal to erect a model farm on Thompson's Island in order to recreate a puritanical atmosphere. Lovell's, Gallop's, Rainsford and the Brewster Islands could be used for camping, clambakes, and outdoor recreation. Complete restoration of Fort Warren has also been proposed. Whether anything will develop out of these proposals remains to be seen. Regardless of what the future brings, however, the islands of Boston Harbor are unique in their heritage and overwhelming in their natural beauty. They should be preserved as national landmarks as well as a wildlife refuge.

BIBLIOGRAPHY

Adams, Charles Francis, *Three Episodes of Massachusetts History*, Vol. I, Boston, Houghton Mifflin Co., 1892.

American Heritage, Editors of, *The American Heritage Picture History of the Civil War*, New York, American Heritage, 1960.

Campbell, J., *Boston Newsletter*, Boston, B. Green, Newbury Street, July 14, 1726.

Coast Guard, U.S., *Historically Famous Lighthouses*, Washington, D.C., Public Information Division, 1957.

Connelly, Patrick Joseph, *The Islands of Boston Harbor*, Boston, Sheldon Press Co., 1936.

Current, R. N., Freidel, F., and Williams, T. H., *American History—A Survey*, 2nd ed., Toronto, Alfred A. Knopf Inc., 1967.

Homans, I. Smith, *History of Boston, 1630–1856*, Boston, F. C. Moore & Co., 1856.

Humphrey, Zephine, *A Book of New England*, New York, Howell, Soskin, 1947.

Krout, John A., *United States to 1865*, New York, Barnes & Noble Inc., 1962.

Loughran, William J., "The Biggest Little Battle," *Yankee Magazine*, Vol. 35, No. 6, p. 94, June 1971.

Mass. Metropolitan Area Planning Council, Vol. 2, 1967.

Murphy, J. F., *Tourist's Guide to Down the Harbor*, J. F. Murphy.

Rideing, William H., "The Gateway of Boston," *Harper's Magazine*, August 1884, p. 352–361.

Rutman, Darrett, *Winthrop's Boston—Portrait of a Puritan Town 1630–1649*, Chapel Hill, University of North Carolina Press, 1965.

Seaburg, Carl, *Boston Observed*, Boston, Beacon Press, 1971.

Shaw, Charles, *Topographical and Historical Description of Boston*, Boston, Oliver Spear, 1817.

Shurtleff, Nathaniel, *Topographical and Historical Description of Boston*, Boston, Rockwell and Churchill, 1891.

Snow, Edward Rowe, *The Islands of Boston Harbor—History and Romance*, Boston, Yankee Publishing Co., 1935.

Snow, Edward Rowe, *The Islands of Boston Harbor, 1630–1971*, New York, Dodd, Mead & Co., 1971.

Snow, Edward Rowe, *Romance of Boston Bay*, Boston, Yankee Publishing Co., 1944.

Snow, Edward Rowe, "The Roving Skeleton of Boston Bay," *Mysterious New England*, Dublin, New Hampshire, Yankee, Inc., 1971.

Snow, Edward Rowe, *Sailing Down Boston Bay*, Boston, Boston Printing Co., 1941.

Snow, Edward Rowe, *True Tales of Buried Treasure*, London, Alvin Redman Ltd., 1963.

Stanley, Raymond W., *The Four Thompsons of Boston Harbor 1621–1965*, 1966.

Stark, James H., *Illustrated History of Boston Harbor*, Boston, Photo-Electrotype Co., 1879.

Stark, James H., *Stark's Antique Views of the Towne of Boston*, Boston, James H. Stark, 1901.

Sweetser, Moses Foster, *King's Handbook of Boston Harbor*, Cambridge, Moses King Corp., 1882.

Taylor, Ralph C., M.A. (Editor-in-Chief) *The New American Encyclopedia*, Boston, New York, Books, Inc., 1938.

Thoreau, Henry David, *Cape Cod*, New York, Thomas Y. Crowell Co., 1961.

Whitehill, Walter Muir, *Boston—A Topographical History*, 2nd ed., Cambridge, Belknap Press of Harvard University Press, 1968.

Winsor, Justin, *The Memorial History of Boston 1630–1880*, Boston, James R. Osgood, Ticknor & Co., 1880.

INDEX

125